STEP·BY·STEP
MEXICAN
Cooking

KÖNEMANN

BASIC MEXICAN PANTRY

Most ingredients for Mexican cooking are familiar and readily available. The exceptions are maizemeal, ready-made tortillas and fresh jalapeno chillies, which are only available at specialty outlets.

Avocado: Pear-shaped fruit with a dark green or purple to black skin. The flesh has a slightly nutty flavour and is creamy yellow-green in colour. Usually eaten raw in salads or mashed and made into a dip. Mexicans generally use the purple-skinned avocados which are often creamier and have more flavour.

Capsicum: Also known as sweet peppers, capsicums are used extensively in Mexican cuisine. There are many varieties, ranging from sweet in flavour to hot. Red capsicums are usually charred under a hot grill, until their skin turns black. They are covered with a tea-towel then skin is removed.

Chillies: Available fresh, dried or powdered. Used lavishly in Mexican cooking. Adjust the amounts in these recipes to suit your palate. Fresh chillies are generally hotter than dried.

Jalapeno Chillies: Ranging from hot to very hot in flavour, jalapeno chillies are dark green in colour and short and stumpy in shape. They can be bought fresh at the greengrocer or in jars at the supermarket. If unavailable substitute small hot red chillies.

Cinnamon: A favourite flavouring in Mexico and used in both sweet and savoury dishes. Available as sticks or in powdered form.

Cloves: An aromatic flavouring used in sweet and savoury dishes, in bud or powdered form.

Coriander: Also known as Cilantro and Chinese parsley. Coriander is used for its refreshing flavour and is available in fresh, seed or powdered form. These are not interchangeable however; fresh coriander has a totally different taste from dried coriander.

Corn: Mexicans use both fresh and dried corn, often referred to as maize. Buy fresh corn on the cob at the greengrocers or in frozen or canned form at the supermarket. Corn on the cob is at its best when cooked straight after it is picked. Most of us will never taste it this fresh, but when buying corn, look for

soft, flexible husks with a bright colour. Avoid buying husked corn wrapped in plastic if you can.

Cumin: Used in seed or powdered form, it has a somewhat bitter, pungent flavour.

Flat plate: A thin earthenware plate used for cooking tortillas. A heavy-based pan may be substituted.

Huevos: Another name for eggs. Huevos Rancheros means 'ranch' or 'country-style' eggs.

Lard: Pork fat. Lard is commonly used in Mexican cookery, but we have chosen olive oil for our recipes as a healthier alternative. If you prefer its flavour, you may wish to substitute lard.

Maizemeal: 'Masa Harina' in Mexico. Finely ground corn used for making tortillas and other baked products. Pale yellow in colour, maizemeal may be purchased in health food shops. It is sometimes referred to as cornmeal but it is not the same as polenta or cornflour.

Onions: Mexicans prefer white onions for their sharper flavour but the milder Spanish or red onions are sometimes used as well (see recipes).

Pepitas: Pumpkin seeds with the skin removed. Green in colour, they may be bought from supermarkets or health food shops.

Refried Beans: Kidney beans fried to an almost paste-like consistency. Sold in cans and available from supermarkets. You can make your own by frying canned and drained red kidney beans (or soaked and cooked dried red kidney beans) in oil or lard, mashing them with a potato masher. They are ready when they start to become crisp at the edges.

Snapper: This fish is a favourite in Mexican cookery. Reddish in colour, with a distinctive bump on the head. Look for firm flesh and bright bulging eyes.

Tacos: Tortillas which have been folded and fried until crisp. Ready-made tacos are sold in supermarkets.

Tortillas: Very popular paper-thin flat breads made from maizemeal in a variety of sizes, depending on their use (see page 8 for recipe).

STEP-BY-STEP MEXICAN COOKING

Cut avocado in half and remove seed with the blade of a sharp knife.

Peel avocado and mash flesh in a bowl using a fork.

STEP-BY-STEP MEXICAN COOKING

STARTERS & SOUPS

Nearly all Mexican food has a 'bite' to it, owing to the liberal use of chillies. These starters and soups are designed to set your taste buds tingling.

Guacamole

A favourite dip.

Preparation time:
  20 minutes
Cooking time:
  Nil
Serves 6

2 ripe avocados
1 small onion
1 medium tomato
1 tablespoon chopped fresh coriander
1/4 cup sour cream
1 tablespoon lemon juice
Tabasco, to taste

1 Cut avocados in half and remove the seed with the blade of a sharp knife.
2 Peel avocados and place flesh in medium bowl. Mash well with a fork until smooth.
3 Finely chop the onion and tomato and mix with chopped fresh coriander.
4 Add to avocado in bowl with remaining ingredients and mix well. Serve as a dip with corn chips or as one of the filling mixtures for tacos.
Note: Avocado flesh discolours when exposed to the air. To help prevent this, bury an avocado seed in the dip and cover with plastic wrap.

HINT
To remove seed without damaging avocado flesh, insert the blade of a sharp knife into the seed. Pull the knife away and the seed will come with it.
Guacamole Melt makes a delicious snack or breakfast dish. Pile Guacamole onto toast, sprinkle with grated cheese and crumbled grilled bacon and grill until the cheese melts.

Finely chop onion, tomato and coriander. Squeeze 1 tablespoons lemon juice.

Mix together all ingredients in a bowl and serve as a dip with corn chips.

Toasted Pepita Dip with Crispy Crackle

Preparation time:
30 minutes
Cooking time:
30-40 minutes
Serves 4-6

1 large piece pork rind
¼ teaspoon chilli powder
½ teaspoon salt

TOASTED PEPITA DIP
1 cup pepitas (see Note)
1 clove garlic
1 medium onion, roughly chopped
2 teaspoons lemon juice
⅓ cup olive oil

1 Preheat oven to 250°C. Line two 32 x 28 cm oven trays with foil. Score pork rind diagonally with sharp-bladed knife.
2 Combine chilli and salt in a small bowl. Rub mixture into pork rind. Place on one prepared tray. Bake for 30 minutes or until crisp. Remove, cool slightly and break into pieces.
3 To make Pepita Dip: Place pepitas on second prepared oven tray. Toast under hot grill 2 minutes until the seeds swell and pop; remove and cool.
4 Place pepitas, garlic, onion, lemon juice and oil into food processor bowl. Process 30 seconds or until smooth. Serve with Crispy Crackle.
Note: Pepitas are shelled pumpkin seeds. They are available in supermarkets and health food stores and sometimes they are simply labelled 'pumpkin seeds'. They are green. Don't confuse them with the white-coloured salted pumpkin seeds – these have to be shelled before they can be eaten. Dip keeps well in the refrigerator. It is equally good served with vegetable sticks.

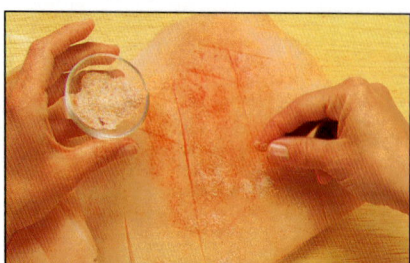

Mix together chilli powder and salt and rub well into scored pork rind.

Bake pork rind for 30 minutes or until crisp. When cool, break into pieces.

STARTERS & SOUPS

Place all ingredients for Pepita Dip into food processor bowl.

Process Pepita Dip until smooth and serve with Crispy Crackle.

Tortillas

Mexican bread, tortillas are served with most meals.

> 1½ cups plain flour, sifted
> 1 cup maizemeal, sifted
> 1 cup warm water

1 Combine flour and maizemeal in a large mixing bowl. Make a well in the centre; gradually add warm water. Using a flat-bladed knife, mix to a firm dough. Turn dough onto lightly floured surface. Knead dough for about 3 minutes or until smooth.

Preparation time:
1 hour
Cooking time:
20 minutes
Makes 16 x 20 cm or 20 x 15 cm or 40 x 10 cm tortillas

2 Divide dough into required portions. Roll out one portion at a time on a lightly floured surface until very thin (about paper thickness). Set aside and repeat with remaining portions. Keep the unrolled portions wrapped in plastic wrap to prevent them from drying out.
3 Heat a dry heavy-based pan or flat plate. Place one tortilla in the dry pan. When the edges begin to curl slightly, turn and cook other side. A few seconds each side is ample cooking time. If residual flour begins to burn in the pan, wipe out with absorbent paper.
Note: Tortillas will soften on standing. Tear into pieces and serve with dips or roll up with filling for a Burrito. Tortillas will keep fresh for a week in an airtight container. Warm them briefly in the oven or microwave. Stale tortillas can be torn or cut into bite-size pieces and fried in lard or oil until crisp. Use them as you would corn chips, with dip. Pronounced *tort-ee-yah*.

Combine flour and maizemeal in a bowl, make a well in centre and add water.

Knead dough on lightly floured surface for 3 minutes until smooth.

STARTERS & SOUPS

Divide dough into portions and roll out to desired size very thinly.

Cook tortillas one at a time on both sides in a dry frying pan or flat plate.

Huevos Rancheros

Preparation time:
 1 hour
Cooking time:
 35 minutes
Serves 6

---

2 small red capsicums, halved and seeded
2 teaspoons olive oil
2 teaspoons olive oil, extra
1 teaspoon ground oregano
1 small onion, finely chopped
1 green capsicum, finely chopped
2 tablespoons tomato paste
2 pickled jalapeno chillies, finely sliced
6 x 15 cm tortillas
6 eggs, fried or poached
1/2 cup grated Cheddar cheese

---

1 Brush capsicums with oil. Grill 12-15 minutes or until skin is black. Cover with damp tea-towel until cool. Peel off skin. Place capsicum flesh in food processor bowl. Process 30 seconds or until smooth. Set aside.
2 Heat extra oil in medium pan. Add oregano, onion, green capsicum and tomato paste. Cook until soft. Stir in red capsicum purée and chillies. Heat gently, stirring 1 minute.
3 To serve, place one fried or poached egg onto a tortilla. Top with a tablespoon of capsicum sauce and sprinkle with the grated Cheddar.
Note: Mexicans eat Huevos Rancheros for breakfast or lunch. Usually served hot, it may also be eaten cold. The capsicum sauce may be used as a dip with tortillas. It also serves as a fiery accompaniment to scrambled eggs or meat dishes. Store the sauce, well covered, in the refrigerator. It will keep fresh for several days.

Cover blackened capsicums with a clean tea-towel until cool.

Peel off the black skin and purée the flesh in a food processor.

STARTERS & SOUPS

Stir red capsicum purée and sliced chillies into sauce and heat for 1 minute.

Place egg on tortilla, top with capsicum sauce and sprinkle with grated cheese.

Chicken and Pea Soup

Preparation time:
  1 hour
Cooking time:
  40 minutes
Serves 6-8

> *1 cup yellow split peas*
> *1/2 cup green split peas*
> *1 small onion, chopped*
> *2 bay leaves*
> *10 peppercorns*
> *1 L water*
> *2 chicken breast fillets*
> *2 cups chicken stock*
> *1 tablespoon chopped fresh coriander*

1 Combine split peas, onion, bay leaves, peppercorns and water in a large pan. Bring to boil, stirring occasionally. Reduce heat and simmer uncovered until peas are soft. Skim the top while simmering to remove surface froth. Remove from heat, cool. Remove and discard bay leaves.
2 Trim chicken of excess fat. Heat chicken stock in pan. Poach chicken fillets until tender. Drain and reserve stock. Cut cooled chicken into very thin strips and set aside.
3 Pour split pea mixture into food processor bowl. Process 1-2 minutes or until smooth. Return mixture to pan. Add chicken, reserved stock and coriander. Heat through and serve.

Note: The soup may be made several hours before it is needed. Reheat gently just before serving. Lentils may be used in this recipe instead of the split peas. They cook faster and if you use red lentils there is no need to soak them overnight first.

Hint
The split peas will cook faster if you soak them in cold water overnight. Do not add salt. Drain and cover with fresh water to cook.

Combine split peas, onion, bay leaves, peppercorns and water in a large pan.

Skim the top of the soup while it is simmering to remove surface froth.

STARTERS & SOUPS

Poach chicken fillets until tender, cool and cut into thin strips.

Purée split pea mixture and add chicken, stock and chopped fresh coriander.

13

Creamy Corn and Tomato Soup

Preparation time:
   35 minutes
Cooking time:
   15 minutes
Serves 4-6

1 teaspoon olive oil
1 teaspoon chicken stock powder
1 medium onion, finely chopped
3 medium tomatoes
1 x 425 g can tomato purée
1 x 310 g can creamed corn
1 x 125 g can corn kernels, drained
chilli powder, to taste
sour cream and tortillas, to serve

1 Heat oil in large pan. Add stock powder and onions, cook until soft.

2 Peel tomatoes, remove seeds with a spoon and chop flesh. Add to pan with tomato purée, creamed corn and corn kernels. Season with chilli. Stir until heated through. Serve with a dollop of sour cream and tortillas.

Note: This soup may be frozen in an airtight container for up to 4 weeks. Keep all the ingredients in your pantry so that you can make up this quick soup anytime.

Heat oil, add onions and stock powder and cook until soft.

Peel tomatoes, cut in half and remove the seeds with a teaspoon.

Add chopped tomatoes to onions in pan with tomato purée and creamed corn.

Add corn kernels, season with chilli and cook until heated through.

STARTERS & SOUPS

Step-By-Step Mexican Cooking

Trim lamb of excess fat and sinew, roll up and tie it securely with string.

Mix together tomato paste, chilli powder, pepper, garlic, cumin and cinnamon.

LAMB, BEEF & PORK

Mexican meat dishes are spicy and tasty, with the warm flavours of cinnamon and cumin predominating.

Roasted Lamb with Chilli

Preparation time:
  15 minutes
Cooking time:
  35 minutes
Serves 4

450 g boneless rib lamb roast
1/4 cup tomato paste
1/4 teaspoon chilli powder
1/4 teaspoon ground pepper
2 cloves garlic, crushed
1 teaspoon ground cumin
1/2 teaspoon ground cinnamon
1/4 cup grated Cheddar cheese

1 Preheat oven to 180°C. Trim meat of excess fat. Roll the meat and tie it securely with string.
2 Combine tomato paste, chilli powder, pepper, garlic, cumin and cinnamon in a small bowl. Spread this mixture all over the meat. Sprinkle with cheese.
3 Place into a baking dish and roast lamb for 35 minutes or until browned and cooked through. Stand, covered with foil for 10 minutes before slicing. Serve with refried beans or fresh vegetables in season.
Note: Lamb cooked with spices in this way is also excellent served cold accompanied by a mixed green salad and warmed tortillas.

Hint
Keep a special board for chopping onion, garlic and chilli.

Spread the chilli mixture all over the meat with a spatula or knife.

Place lamb in a baking dish and sprinkle with grated Cheddar cheese.

Lamb Empanados

Mexico's meat pie.

Preparation time:
1 hour
Cooking time:
30 minutes
Serves 6

---

2 teaspoons olive oil
250 g minced lamb
1/2 small onion, finely chopped
1/2 medium green capsicum, finely chopped
1 small carrot, finely chopped
2 tablespoons tomato paste
1 teaspoon ground cinnamon
2 teaspoons brown sugar

PASTRY
2 cups self-raising flour, sifted
250 g butter, chopped
1 egg
1/4 cup water
30 g butter, extra, softened
1 egg yolk, lightly beaten

---

1 Heat oil in a medium pan; add mince and onion, cook over medium-high heat 3 minutes. Add capsicum, carrot, tomato paste, cinnamon and sugar. Mix well. Remove from heat, cool.

2 Preheat oven to 200°C. Brush a 32 x 28 cm oven tray with melted butter or oil. Dust with flour. Shake off excess.

3 To make Pastry: Place flour and butter in food processor bowl. Process 30 seconds or until mixture has a fine crumbly texture. Add egg and water. Process 30 seconds or until mixture comes together. Turn dough onto a lightly floured surface. Knead until smooth. Be careful not to handle too much or the dough will become sticky. Divide into three equal portions.

4 On a lightly floured surface, roll each portion into a 20 x 20 cm square. Spread two of the squares with extra butter. Stack all three dough squares on top of each other, with the unbuttered square on top. Roll out the layers together.

5 To Assemble: Cut out six 15 cm circles from pastry. Divide meat mixture evenly between the circles. Brush edges with egg yolk. Fold in half, pressing edges together. Place on prepared tray, brush with egg yolk and bake 15 minutes or until puffed and golden. Serve with a green salad.

Note: Freeze Empanados in an airtight plastic bag for 4 weeks. Mexicans use any kind of savoury filling in these turnovers. Try making them with taco filling.

Lamb, Beef & Pork

Add capsicum, carrot, tomato paste, cinnamon and sugar to cooked lamb.

Divide dough into 3 equal portions and roll each portion into a square.

Spread two dough squares with butter and stack squares on top of each other.

Place spoonfuls of filling on each dough circle, brush edge with egg and fold.

19

Tex Mex Chilli con Carne

Preparation time:
   30 minutes
Cooking time:
   40 minutes
Serves 4

---

1 tablespoon olive oil
2 cloves garlic, crushed
750 g lean round steak, cut into 2 cm cubes
1 large onion, chopped
2 bay leaves
1 cup tomato juice
1 x 440 g can tomatoes, crushed
1 x 465 g can red kidney beans, drained
½ teaspoon ground oregano
1 teaspoon ground cumin
½ teaspoon chilli powder

---

1 Heat oil and garlic in a large pan. Cook meat in batches over medium heat until well browned.
2 Add onion, bay leaves, tomato juice and tomatoes. Stir, and bring to the boil; reduce heat.
3 Simmer covered until meat is very soft and liquid has reduced by half. Stir in kidney beans and spices and heat. Serve with Guacamole and corn chips.

Cook cubed meat in oil flavoured with garlic in batches until well browned.

Add onion, bay leaves, tomato juice and tomatoes to meat in pan.

When meat is very soft and liquid has reduced, stir in kidney beans.

At the last minute stir in oregano, cumin and chilli powder, heat and serve.

LAMB, BEEF & PORK

21

Step-by-Step Mexican Cooking

Spicy Beef and Bean Tacos

Preparation time:
  25 minutes
Cooking time:
  15 minutes
Serves 4

---

2 teaspoons olive oil
250 g minced beef
1 small onion, finely chopped
1/4 teaspoon chilli powder
1/4 cup tomato paste
1 teaspoon ground cumin
1 teaspoon ground coriander
1 x 450 g can refried beans
12 taco shells
1/2 cup grated Cheddar cheese
2 small carrots, grated
2 medium tomatoes, sliced
1/2 small lettuce, shredded

---

1 Heat oil in medium pan; add mince and onion. Cook over medium-high heat 3 minutes until well browned and almost all the liquid has evaporated.

2 Add chilli, tomato paste, cumin, coriander and refried beans. Mix well. Cook, stirring occasionally, for 2-3 minutes or until mixture is hot.

3 To serve, preheat oven to 180°C. Place taco shells over the rungs of the oven rack. This will prevent them from closing up while they heat. Heat for about 8 minutes until they are crisp. Alternatively, taco shells can be heated in a microwave oven. Follow instructions on the packet. Fill shells with mince mixture, cheese, carrots, tomatoes and lettuce. Sour cream or Guacamole can also be added if liked.

Note: Mince mixture can be made and frozen for 4 weeks in an airtight container. Taco shells also freeze well. They do not have to be thawed before reheating.

Cook minced beef and chopped onion in oil until meat is well browned.

Add chilli powder, tomato paste, cumin and coriander and stir in well.

LAMB, BEEF & PORK

Stir in refried beans and cook for 2-3 minutes or until mixture is hot.

Place meat mixture in taco shells and top with cheese, carrots, tomato and lettuce.

STEP-BY-STEP MEXICAN COOKING

Burritos

Serve hot or cold.

Preparation time:
15 minutes
Cooking time:
30 minutes
Serves 4

500 g rump steak
1 teaspoon olive oil
1 medium onion,
finely sliced
1 cinnamon stick
4 cloves
1 bay leaf
2 cups beef stock
8 x 20 cm tortillas
Tomato Salsa, to
serve

1 Trim meat of excess fat; cut into 2 cm cubes. Heat oil in a medium pan, add onion. Cook until golden brown.
2 Add meat, cinnamon stick, cloves, bay leaf and beef stock. Bring to boil. Reduce heat, simmer covered for 30 minutes or until meat is soft and liquid is almost all absorbed. Remove and discard the cinnamon stick, cloves and bay leaf.
3 Shred meat with two forks. Serve rolled up in a tortilla with Tomato Salsa and salad.

Note: The meat mixture will keep, covered, in the refrigerator for up to one week.

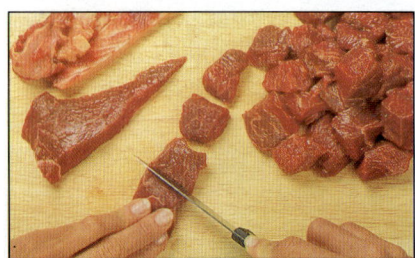
Trim meat of excess fat and sinew. Cut into 2 cm cubes.

Cook sliced onion in oil over medium heat until golden brown.

Add meat to pan with cinnamon stick, cloves, bay leaf and beef stock.

When meat is cooked and liquid almost absorbed, shred meat with two forks.

LAMB, BEEF & PORK

Pork Ribs with Tomato and Pineapple

Preparation time:
30 minutes
Cooking time:
30 minutes
Serves 4-6

---

2 teaspoons coriander seeds, crushed (see Note)
1 teaspoon cumin seeds, crushed
1/2 cup plain flour, sifted
600 g pork spare ribs, cut into 4 cm pieces
1 tablespoon olive oil
1 medium onion, chopped
2 x 440 g cans tomatoes, crushed
1 tablespoon tomato paste
2 medium zucchini, sliced
1 small pineapple, skinned and cut into small wedges

---

1 Combine crushed coriander seeds, cumin seeds and flour in a medium bowl. Dust pork ribs with this spiced flour mixture; shake off excess. Reserve 2 teaspoons of spiced flour mixture. Sift remaining spiced flour mixture, discard flour and add spices to reserved spiced flour mixture.

2 Heat oil in a large pan. Cook meat in batches over medium-high heat until well browned. Drain on absorbent paper. Add onion and cook until soft. Add reserved spiced flour mixture; stir over low heat.

3 Add tomatoes and tomato paste, stir to combine. Bring to boil and allow to thicken, stirring constantly. Return pork to pan. Add zucchini and pineapple. Cook a further 10 minutes or until meat and zucchini are tender.

Note: Crushing your own seeds releases a fresher, more pungent flavour. Use a mortar and pestle or coffee grinder. If not available, ready-ground spices may be substituted.

Crush coriander seeds and cumin seeds in a mortar and pestle.

Dust pork ribs in spiced flour and cook in batches in oil until well browned.

Add tomatoes and tomato paste to cooked onion in pan.

Return pork to pan, add zucchini and pineapple and cook until tender.

STEP-BY-STEP MEXICAN COOKING

Mix together tomato, onion, tomato paste, cumin, coriander and Tabasco.

Brush fish with a mixture of pepper, lemon juice and melted butter.

SEAFOOD

Mexicans love seafood and these tasty fish and shellfish dishes are fresh, simple to prepare and very quick.

Bream with Tomato Cheese Crust

Preparation time:
  40 minutes
Cooking time:
  15 minutes
Serves 4

2 medium ripe tomatoes, peeled, seeded, finely chopped
1 small onion, finely chopped
1 tablespoon tomato paste
1/2 teaspoon ground cumin
1/2 teaspoon ground coriander
Tabasco, to taste
1/4 teaspoon ground pepper
1 tablespoon lemon juice
20 g butter, melted
4 medium bream fillets
3/4 cup grated Cheddar cheese
1/2 cup fresh breadcrumbs

1 Preheat oven to 180°C. Brush a 32 x 28 cm oven tray with melted butter or oil. Place chopped tomato in a small bowl. Add onion, tomato paste, cumin, coriander and Tabasco. Mix well, and set aside.

2 Combine pepper, lemon juice and butter in a separate small bowl. Place bream fillets on prepared tray. Brush each fillet with pepper mixture and top with tomato mixture.

3 Sprinkle with combined cheese and breadcrumbs. Bake 15 minutes or until tender and fish flakes when tested with a fork. Serve hot with accompanying salads and warmed tortilla.

Top fish with tomato mixture and sprinkle with combined cheese and breadcrumbs.

To test fish, insert a fork into thickest part. If it flakes it is cooked.

Baked Snapper with Bacon and Capers

Preparation time:
  25 minutes
Cooking time:
  40 minutes
Serves 4-6

---

4 small snapper
  (about 300 g each)
lemon juice, to taste
ground pepper, to
  taste
1 teaspoon olive oil
1 small onion, thinly
  sliced
2 rashers bacon,
  finely chopped
1/4 cup white wine
1 tablespoon capers
2 tablespoons sour
  cream
1/2 cup cream

---

1 Preheat oven to 180°C. Scale and clean fish. Place fish side-by-side in an ovenproof dish. Sprinkle fish with lemon juice and pepper, set aside.

2 Heat oil in a small pan, add onion and bacon. Cook until onion is soft. Stir in wine, capers, sour cream and cream. Pour over fish. Bake 40 minutes. Serve with vegetables or a green salad.

Note: Small bream may be used instead of snapper or try this sauce over any of your favourite small whole fish.

Place fish in an ovenproof dish, pour over lemon juice and sprinkle with pepper.

Cook onions and bacon in oil until the onion is soft.

Stir in wine, capers, sour cream and cream. Mix well.

Pour the sauce over fish, and bake for 40 minutes or until cooked.

Seafood

Prawns in Coriander

Preparation time:
  25 minutes
Cooking time:
  10 minutes
Serves 4–6

---

24 green king prawns
40 g butter
1 clove garlic, crushed
2 teaspoons brown sugar
2 tablespoons lime juice
3 tablespoons chopped fresh coriander
2 teaspoons chopped fresh chives
2 teaspoons sour cream

---

1 Shell prawns, leaving tails intact; devein. Set aside.
2 Heat butter in a medium pan, add garlic, sugar, lime juice, coriander, chives and sour cream. Mix well. Add prawns, toss through until pinkish in colour and tender. Serve hot or cold.

Note: Oysters and other shellfish may also be cooked in the same way.
Coriander is a pungent herb and often used in Mexican cooking. It is an acquired taste so it's best not to make this dish for guests unless you are sure that they like coriander.

Shell green king prawns, leaving their tails intact. Remove veins.

Heat butter in pan, add garlic, sugar, lime juice, coriander, chives and sour cream.

Once the sauce is hot and well mixed, add the prawns.

Cook the prawns, stirring constantly, just until they turn pink. Do not overcook.

Seafood

Spicy Seafood and Rice

Preparation time:
45 minutes
Cooking time:
20 minutes
Serves 4-6

1½ cups vegetable or fish stock
10 mussels, scrubbed
2 medium calamari hoods, sliced
10 medium green prawns, shelled and deveined
1 tablespoon olive oil
½ teaspoon ground cinnamon
½ teaspoon ground cloves
1 medium onion, finely chopped
¼ cup tomato paste
1½ cups long-grain rice
1½ cups water
1 x 240 g can baby clams, drained
lime juice, to taste

---

1 Place stock in a medium pan. Bring to boil, reduce heat and add mussels, calamari and prawns. Simmer until mussel shells have opened and calamari and prawns are just tender. Remove with a slotted spoon, set aside and reserve stock. Discard any mussels that haven't opened.
2 Heat oil in a large pan. Add cinnamon, cloves, onion and tomato paste; stir over medium heat. Add rice, reduce heat to low. Stir rice 2 minutes or until lightly golden.
3 Combine reserved stock and water. Add a quarter of combined liquid to the pan. Stir continuously for 4-5 minutes or until liquid is absorbed.
4 Repeat this process 3 times, stirring continuously, until all the liquid has been added and the rice is almost tender.
5 Add poached seafood and clams. Stir in a little lime juice. Cover and stand for 4 minutes. Serve immediately with Tomato Salsa and warmed tortillas torn into pieces.

Mussels are cooked when their shells have opened. Discard unopened mussels.

Add cinnamon, cloves, onion, tomato paste and rice to oil in pan.

SEAFOOD

Add one-quarter of liquid to pan and cook until liquid is absorbed. Repeat process.

When rice is tender, add poached seafood, clams and lime juice.

35

STEP-BY-STEP MEXICAN COOKING

Combine garlic, allspice, oregano, cumin, cinnamon, chilli, coriander and wine.

Pour spice mixture over chicken breast fillets, cover and refrigerate.

CHICKEN

Chicken cooked the Mexican way is, for most of us, a new experience – especially its unusual and surprisingly delicious combination with chocolate.

Spiced Chicken Fillets

Adjust chilli to taste.

Preparation time:
30 minutes +
4 hours marinating
Cooking time:
30-40 minutes
Serves 4

6 cloves garlic
1/2 teaspoon ground allspice
1 teaspoon oregano
1/2 teaspoon ground cinnamon
1/2 teaspoon chilli powder
1 teaspoon ground cumin
1/2 teaspoon ground coriander
1/3 cup red wine
4 chicken breast fillets
60 g ghee, for frying

1 Place garlic, allspice, oregano, cinnamon, chilli, cumin, coriander and wine in a food processor. Process 1-2 minutes or until smooth. Set aside.
2 Place chicken in a medium bowl. Pour over spice mixture. Cover and refrigerate for 4 hours.
3 Heat ghee in large pan. Drain marinade from chicken. Cook chicken in batches over medium-high heat 5-7 minutes or until tender, turning once. Serve with fresh vegetables.

Note: Allspice is also called Jamaica pepper because most of the world's allspice comes from Jamaica. It is the dried berry of a tree native to tropical America, and is called allspice because its taste resembles a mixture of several spices.

Drain chicken from marinade, heat ghee and fry chicken in batches.

Cook chicken 5-7 minutes or until tender, turning once.

Fruity Baked Chicken

Preparation time:
  25 minutes
Cooking time:
  30-40 minutes
Serves 4

STUFFING
1 teaspoon lemon juice
1 small onion, chopped
200 g dried fruit salad, chopped
20 g butter, melted
½ cup flaked almonds
ground pepper, to taste
½ teaspoon ground cumin

1 x 1.3 kg chicken
½ teaspoon ground pepper, extra
½ teaspoon ground cumin, extra
1 tablespoon lemon juice, extra
30 g butter, melted, extra

1 Preheat oven to 180°C. Combine lemon juice, onion, dried fruit, butter, almonds, pepper and cumin in a small mixing bowl. Trim chicken of excess fat, place stuffing in chicken cavity and tie wings and drumsticks securely into place with string.
2 Combine extra pepper, cumin, lemon juice and butter in a small bowl. Brush mixture over chicken. Place onto roasting rack over oven tray. Roast for 30-40 minutes or until golden brown and cooked through. Allow to stand covered with foil 10 minutes and remove string before serving. Serve with the fruit stuffing and fresh vegetables.
Note: If preferred, dried apricots may be substituted for the dried fruit salad.

HINT
Butter a slice of stale bread and place it, butter-side-in, in the opening of the chicken. This will keep the stuffing in place.

Combine all stuffing ingredients in a small bowl and mix well.

Place stuffing mixture into chicken cavity and tie wings and drumsticks with string.

CHICKEN

Mix together pepper, cumin, lemon juice and melted butter.

Brush this mixture all over the chicken, place on roasting rack and bake.

Chicken in Capsicum Sauce

Preparation time:
  25 minutes
Cooking time:
  30-40 minutes
Serves 4

---

2 medium red capsicums, halved and seeded (see Note)
2 teaspoons olive oil
1 tablespoon olive oil, extra
1 kg chicken pieces
1 medium onion, finely chopped
2 cloves garlic, crushed
2 green apples, peeled and grated
1 teaspoon ground oregano
1 x 440 g can tomatoes, crushed
2 medium yellow or red capsicums, extra, seeded and sliced
chilli powder to taste, optional

---

1 Brush red capsicums with oil. Grill 12-15 minutes or until skin is black. Cover with damp tea-towel until cool. Peel off skin. Place capsicums in a food processor bowl. Process 30 seconds or until mixture is smooth. Set aside.

2 Heat oil in frypan. Cook chicken in batches over medium-high heat 5 minutes or until golden brown, turning once. Remove from pan; drain on absorbent paper.

3 Add onion, garlic, apple and oregano to pan and stir over low heat. Add tomatoes, red capsicum purée and capsicum slices, stirring for 2 minutes. Return chicken pieces to pan. Bring to boil, reduce heat. Simmer uncovered for 40 minutes or until liquid has reduced and chicken is tender. Season with chilli, to taste. Serve with warmed tortillas.

Note: Grilling the red capsicums until the skin blackens and blisters gives the flesh a distinctive smoky flavour.

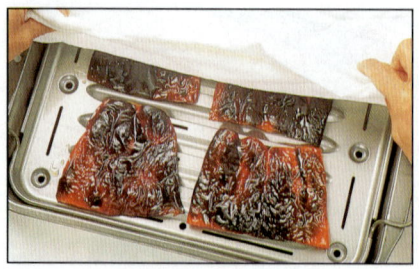

Grill red capsicum halves until skin is black. Cover with damp tea-towel.

Cook chicken pieces in batches for 5 minutes or until golden brown.

CHICKEN

Add onion, garlic, apple and oregano to pan and cook over low heat.

Add tomatoes, red capsicum purée and capsicum slices to onion mixture.

Chicken in Chocolate Sauce

Preparation time:
  20 minutes
Cooking time:
  20 minutes
Serves 4

1/2 cup plain flour, sifted
1/4 teaspoon ground cinnamon
4 chicken breast fillets
2 teaspoons olive oil
20 g butter
1 small onion, finely sliced
2 teaspoons cocoa powder, sifted
2 teaspoons brown sugar
2 teaspoons tomato paste
1/4 cup red wine
1 cup chicken stock
1 tablespoon sour cream
1/3 cup raisins
toasted flaked almonds, to garnish

---

1 Preheat oven to 180°C. Combine flour and cinnamon in a medium bowl. Toss chicken fillets lightly in seasoned flour. Shake off excess. Reserve 1 teaspoon of flour mixture. Heat oil and butter in large pan. Cook chicken over medium heat until golden, turning once. Remove from pan; drain on absorbent paper.

2 Add onion, cocoa, sugar and tomato paste to pan and stir over low heat. Add red wine and stock gradually, stirring over low heat until mixture is smooth.

3 Blend sour cream and reserved flour in a small bowl until smooth. Add to onion mixture with raisins, stir over medium heat 2 minutes or until thickened slightly. Remove from heat.

4 Place chicken fillets in an ovenproof baking dish. Pour over sauce. Cover with lid. Bake for 20 minutes or until chicken is tender. Serve chicken sprinkled with toasted flaked almonds.

Toss chicken fillets in seasoned flour then cook in butter and oil until golden.

Add onion, cocoa, sugar and tomato paste, then add wine and stock.

CHICKEN

Blend sour cream and flour until smooth. Add to onion mixture with raisins.

Pour sauce over chicken fillets, cover and bake until tender.

Step-By-Step Mexican Cooking

Heat oil and add onion, tomato paste, chilli, cumin seeds and tomato juice.

Add stock and crushed tomatoes to pan, bring to boil, then reduce the heat.

STEP-BY-STEP MEXICAN COOKING

VEGETABLES & SALADS

Many Mexican vegetable dishes can be served as a main dish with tortillas or as a course on their own.

Combination Vegetable Stew

Preparation time:
30 minutes
Cooking time:
10–15 minutes
Serves 6

2 teaspoons olive oil
1 small onion, thinly sliced
1/4 cup tomato paste
1/4 teaspoon chilli powder
1 teaspoon cumin seeds
1/2 cup tomato juice
1 cup vegetable stock
1 x 440 g can tomatoes, crushed
2 small carrots, sliced
2 medium zucchini, halved and sliced
20 green beans
300 g cauliflower, cut into small florets

1 Heat oil in large pan. Add onion, tomato paste, chilli, cumin seeds and tomato juice. Stir until well combined.
2 Add stock and crushed tomatoes. Bring to boil. Reduce heat. Add remaining vegetables. Simmer uncovered until soft. Serve with fresh tortillas.
Note: Mexicans make this stew with many different vegetable combinations and quite often with leftovers from the previous night. If you use cooked vegetables they will require only a few minutes in the sauce to heat through. Cook the sauce for 10 minutes before adding the vegetables. Sweetcorn, either fresh or canned, is a popular addition throughout Mexico.

Cut vegetables into pieces that will be cooked at the same time.

Add vegetables to tomato sauce in pan and simmer, uncovered, until soft.

Cheesy Rice-stuffed Capsicums

Preparation time:
40 minutes
Cooking time:
25 minutes
Serves 6

---

3 small red capsicums
3 small green capsicums
1 tablespoon olive oil
1 small onion, chopped
1/4 teaspoon chilli powder
1/2 teaspoon ground cumin
1 teaspoon chicken stock powder
2 tablespoons tomato paste
1 cup short-grain rice
2 cups water
1 x 310 g can corn kernels, drained
2 pickled jalapeno chillies, chopped
3/4 cup Cheddar cheese, grated

---

1 Preheat oven to 180°C. Cut tops off capsicums and set aside. Carefully remove pith and seeds, taking care not to tear the capsicum shells open.

2 Heat oil in a medium pan. Stir in onion, chilli powder, cumin, stock powder, tomato paste and rice. Add water. Cover with tight-fitting lid. Bring slowly to boil; stir once. Reduce heat, simmer, covered until almost all water is absorbed. Remove from heat. Stand, covered 5 minutes or until all water is absorbed and rice is just tender. Stir through corn, chillies and 1/2 cup cheese.

3 Fill each capsicum with rice mixture. Sprinkle each with remaining cheese. Replace tops. Place capsicums on oven tray and bake for 15 minutes or until capsicums have softened slightly. Serve warm accompanied by tortillas and salad.
Note: Yellow capsicums may also be used in this recipe.

Cut tops off capsicums and carefully remove pith and seeds.

Heat oil, add onion, chilli powder, cumin, stock powder, tomato paste and rice.

VEGETABLES & SALADS

When rice is tender, stir through corn, chillies and 1/2 cup grated cheese.

Fill each capsicum with rice mixture, sprinkle with cheese and replace tops.

Hot Chilli Corn

A summer starter.

Preparation time:
15 minutes
Cooking time:
10 minutes
Serves 6

3 whole corn cobs, sliced in 3 cm rounds
40 g butter, melted
2 tablespoons chopped fresh coriander
1 tablespoon tomato paste
1/4 teaspoon chilli powder, or to taste
sour cream, to serve

1 Half fill a large pan with water. Bring to the boil and add corn. Reduce heat, simmer until corn is soft. Drain.
2 Combine butter, coriander, tomato paste and chilli in a large bowl. Add hot corn. Mix well. Serve immediately with a dollop of sour cream.

Note: If fresh corn is unavailable, use frozen corn cobs. The combination of corn, coriander and chilli is a startling taste for those of us whose only experience of corn on the cob is with butter and pepper. Very popular in Mexico, it may well become your favourite way to eat fresh corn.

Remove husks from corn on the cob and slice into 3 cm rounds.

Boil up a pan of water, add corn and simmer until corn is tender. Drain.

Mix together melted butter, coriander, tomato paste and chilli powder.

Add hot corn to the chilli mixture and toss well to mix. Serve with sour cream.

Vegetables & Salads

Sweet and Spicy Lentils

Preparation time:
  10 minutes
Cooking time:
  15-20 minutes
Serves 6

¾ cup red lentils
1 small onion, finely chopped
½ teaspoon ground cumin
½ teaspoon ground cinnamon
4 cloves
1 cup orange juice
½ cup water

---

1 Wash and drain the lentils and place them in a medium pan with the onion, cumin, cinnamon, cloves, orange juice and water. Bring to boil. Reduce heat and simmer uncovered, stirring occasionally, until liquid has been absorbed and lentils are very soft. Remove cloves and serve hot or cold with your favourite Mexican meat dish or roll up in a tortilla with or without meat to make a Burrito.

Note: Brown or green lentils may be used in this recipe instead of red ones. However, they take longer to cook as they are large and break down less easily. Overnight soaking will shorten the cooking time.

Prepare the ingredients: chop onion, juice orange and measure spices.

Combine in a pan the lentils, onion, spices, orange juice and water.

Bring mixture to the boil and simmer, uncovered, until liquid is absorbed.

The dish is cooked when the lentils are very soft. Remove cloves before serving.

VEGETABLES & SALADS

51

Avocado with Lime and Chillies

Preparation time:
  20 minutes
Cooking time:
  Nil
Serves 6

---

1 teaspoon finely grated lime rind
2 tablespoons lime juice
1 teaspoon brown sugar
1 tablespoon olive oil
1 tablespoon chopped fresh parsley
2-3 pickled jalapeno chillies, seeded and sliced
2 ripe avocados, peeled and sliced

Thoroughly combine lime rind and juice, sugar, oil, parsley and chillies in a small bowl. Pour over sliced avocado. Serve as a tangy side salad to fish, shellfish, chicken or meat dishes.

Note: This salad will keep for 2-3 days covered in the refrigerator – the lime juice prevents the avocados from browning. If limes are unavailable, use lemons instead. You can also cut the avocado into cubes or make into balls with a melon baller (the avocado must be firm), pour over the dressing as above and serve as an appetiser.

Finely grate the lime rind, seed and slice the chillies and chop the parsley.

Peel avocado, remove seed and cut into even slices.

Mix together the grated lime rind and juice, sugar, oil, parsley and chillies.

Pour sauce over sliced avocado and serve as a side salad.

Vegetables & Salads

Tomato Salsa

A Mexican standard.

Preparation time:
10 minutes
Cooking time:
Nil
Serves 4-6

1 medium tomato, finely chopped
1 medium red onion, finely sliced
2 tablespoons chopped fresh coriander
3 tablespoons lemon juice
2 teaspoons grated lemon rind

Thoroughly combine all ingredients in a medium bowl. Cover and chill in the refrigerator. Serve as an accompaniment to Empanados, a filling for Tacos, wrapped up in a tortilla for Burritos or as a refreshing sauce with meat, chicken or seafood dishes.

Note: Use spring onions if a milder flavour is preferred. Or add a little finely chopped green or red chilli for zest. The size of the tomato and onion will determine the quantity that this recipe makes. It is at its best when eaten fresh, but it can be stored, covered, for up to 2 days in the refrigerator.

Chop the tomato very finely and slice the red onion lengthways.

Finely chop the fresh coriander, squeeze 3 tablespoons lemon juice and grate rind.

Place tomato, onion, coriander and lemon rind in bowl. Add juice.

Stir well to mix, then cover with plastic wrap and chill in refrigerator.

Vegetables & Salads

Step-By-Step Mexican Cooking

DESSERTS & BISCUITS

Mexicans like their desserts spicy rather than sweet. Cinnamon and cloves are the favourites.

Fresh Fruit with Clove Syrup

Preparation time:
 15 minutes
Cooking time:
 15 minutes
Serves 4-6

½ cup brown sugar
¼ cup water
¼ teaspoon ground cloves
1 tablespoon Triple Sec liqueur
⅓ cup lemon juice
1 small pineapple, cut into thin wedges
2 medium bananas, sliced diagonally
2 mangoes, sliced

1 Combine sugar, water, cloves, Triple Sec and lemon juice in a small pan. Stir over low heat until sugar has dissolved. Bring to boil. Reduce heat. Simmer uncovered until liquid has reduced by a quarter.
2 Pour cooled syrup over fruit. Serve with sour cream.

Combine sugar, lemon juice, water, cloves and Triple Sec in a small pan.

Simmer syrup, uncovered, until liquid has reduced by a quarter of its volume.

Cut the fruit into attractive and easy-to-eat pieces.

Arrange the fruit in a serving dish and pour over the cooled syrup.

Creamy Chocolate Cinnamon Ring

Preparation time:
20 minutes +
overnight standing
Cooking time:
40 minutes
Serves 6-8

2/3 cup caster sugar
1/2 teaspoon ground cinnamon
150 g dark chocolate, chopped
1 1/4 cups thickened cream
4 eggs, lightly beaten
1/2 cup milk

---

1 Preheat oven to 150°C. Brush a 20 cm (4 cup) ring tin with melted butter or oil. Place sugar and cinnamon into a medium heavy-based pan; heat gently without stirring until sugar begins to melt. Stir over low heat until evenly coloured and sugar has dissolved. Remove from heat; stand 1 minute. Pour into the base of prepared tin.
2 Combine chocolate and cream in a medium pan. Stir over low heat until chocolate has melted. Remove from heat. Cool slightly.
3 Whisk chocolate mixture, eggs and milk together in a large mixing bowl. Pour mixture into ring tin.
4 Stand filled ring tin in a deep baking dish. Pour in enough warm water to come halfway up the sides. Bake 40 minutes or until custard is set and a sharp knife comes out clean when inserted. Remove tin from water bath immediately.
5 Cool custard in the tin and refrigerate overnight. Run a flat-bladed knife around the edge of the tin. Turn onto a serving plate. If custard sticks to tin, place a hot cloth over the base of upturned tin for a couple of minutes. Serve with slices of fresh seasonal fruits.

Combine sugar and cinnamon in a pan and heat gently until sugar begins to melt.

Whisk eggs and milk into cooled chocolate mixture in bowl.

DESSERTS & BISCUITS

Stand filled ring tin in baking dish and pour warm water into dish.

Custard is set when a sharp knife comes out clean when inserted in the centre.

59

Cinnamon Fritters

Preparation time:
1 hour
Cooking time:
30 minutes
Makes 36

1 cup water
70 g butter
1 cup self-raising flour, sifted
4 eggs, lightly beaten
oil, for deep-frying

CINNAMON SYRUP
1/2 cup brown sugar
1 cup water
2 tablespoons orange juice
1 teaspoon ground cinnamon

1 Combine water and butter in a medium pan. Stir over low heat until butter has melted; do not boil.
2 Remove pan from heat, add flour all at once. Beat until smooth using a wooden spoon. Return to stove, heat until mixture thickens and comes away from side and base of pan. Remove from heat; cool slightly. Transfer mixture to a small mixer bowl. Add beaten eggs gradually, beating well after each addition until mixture is glossy.
3 Heat oil in a deep pan. Gently lower heaped teaspoonful of mixture into moderately hot oil and cook over medium-high heat 5 minutes or until puffed and golden. Remove with slotted spoon. Drain on absorbent paper. Serve warm with Cinnamon Syrup.
4 To make Cinnamon Syrup: Combine brown sugar, water, orange juice and cinnamon in a small pan. Stir until sugar has dissolved. Bring to boil. Reduce heat. Simmer until liquid has reduced to three-quarters of its volume. Serve warm with Cinnamon Fritters.
Note: A little grated orange or lemon rind can be added to the batter if liked.

Add flour all at once to water and butter and beat until smooth.

Add beaten eggs gradually, beating well after each addition.

DESSERTS & BISCUITS

To make Cinnamon Syrup, combine all ingredients in a small pan.

Remove puffed and golden fritters from oil with a slottted spoon.

61

Cinnamon Shortbread Biscuits

Preparation time:
 20 minutes
Cooking time:
 10 minutes
Makes 24

½ cup plain flour
1 cup self-raising flour
½ cup almonds, toasted
¼ cup raw sugar
150 g butter, softened
1 egg
¼ cup caster sugar
½ teaspoon ground cinnamon

1 Preheat oven to 180°C. Brush a 32 x 28 cm oven tray with melted butter or oil, line base with paper; grease paper.
2 Place both flours, almonds, raw sugar, butter and egg in a food processor bowl. Using the pulse action, process for 1 minute or until the mixture comes together into a dough.
3 Form level tablespoonsful of mixture into balls. Flatten the balls between the palms of both hands. Place on prepared tray.
4 Sprinkle biscuits with combined caster sugar and cinnamon. Bake for 10 minutes. Cool on a wire rack before serving.

Process flours, almonds, raw sugar, butter and egg until it forms a dough.

Take level tablespoons of mixture and roll into balls with your hands.

DESSERTS & BISCUITS

Flatten balls between the palms of both hands and place on baking tray.

Mix together caster sugar and cinnamon and sprinkle over unbaked biscuits.

INDEX

Avocado with lime and chillies, 52

Beef and bean tacos, spicy, 22
Bream with tomato cheese crust, 29
Burritos, 24

Capsicum sauce, chicken in, 40
Capsicums, cheesy, rice-stuffed, 46
Cheesy rice-stuffed capsicums, 46
Chicken and pea soup, 12
Chicken fillets, spiced, 37
Chicken in capsicum sauce, 40
Chicken in chocolate sauce, 42
Chicken, fruity, baked, 38
Chilli con carne, tex mex, 20
Chocolate cinnamon ring, creamy, 58
Chocolate sauce, chicken in, 42
Cinnamon fritters, 60
Cinnamon shortbread biscuits, 62
Clove syrup, fresh fruit with, 57

Combination vegetable stew, 45
Corn and tomato soup, creamy, 14
Corn, hot chilli, 48
Creamy chocolate cinnamon ring, 58
Crispy crackle, toasted pepita dip with, 6

Empanados, lamb, 18

Fritters, cinnamon, 60
Fruit with clove syrup, 57
Fruity baked chicken, 38

Guacamole, 5

Hot chilli corn, 48
Huevos Rancheros, 10
Lamb empanados, 18

Lamb, roasted, with chilli, 17
Lentils, sweet and spicy, 50
Lime and chillies, avocado with, 52

Pepita dip, toasted, with crispy crackle, 6
Pork ribs with tomato and pineapple, 26
Prawns in coriander, 32

Salsa, tomato, 54
Shortbread biscuits, cinnamon, 62
Snapper, baked, with bacon and capers, 30
Soup
 Chicken and pea, 12
 Creamy corn and tomato, 14
Spicy seafood and rice, 34
Sweet and spicy lentils, 50

Tacos, spicy beef and bean, 22
Tex mex chilli con carne, 20
Tomato salsa, 54
Tortillas, 8

Vegetable stew, combination, 45